BEST BIBLE STORIES

The Walls That Fell Down Flat

THE WALLS THAT FELL DOWN FLAT

Jennifer Rees Larcombe
Illustrated by Steve Björkman

CROSSWAY BOOKS • WHEATON, ILLINOIS
A DIVISION OF GOOD NEWS PUBLISHERS

The Walls That Fell Down Flat
Text copyright © 1992, 1999 by Jennifer Rees Larcombe
Illustrations copyright © 1999 by Steve Björkman
U. S. edition published 2000 by Crossway Books
a division of Good News Publishers
1300 Crescent Street
Wheaton, Illinois 60187

First British edition published 1992
by Marshall Pickering as part of *Children's Bible Story Book*.
This book published as a separate edition in 1999
by Marshall Pickering, an Imprint of HarperCollins Religious,
part of HarperCollins Publishers,
77-85 Fulham Palace Road, London W6 8JB.

Jennifer Rees Larcombe and Steve Björkman assert the moral right to be
identified as the author and illustrator of this work

Cover design: Cindy Kiple
First U. S. printing 2000
Printed in Hong Kong

ISBN 1-58134-151-2

15 14 13 12 11 10 09 08 07 06 05 04 03 02 01 00
15 14 13 12 11 10 9 8 7 6 5 4 3 2 1

THE WALLS THAT FELL DOWN FLAT

Joshua 6

For **forty years** the people of Canaan had been **worried.**

They knew the Jews were prowling about in the desert, ready to come and take over their land.

"Why are they waiting **so long?**" they asked each other.

Now the Canaanites were very **bad** people.

They were **so scared** of their pretend gods that sometimes they threw people into a fire.

They thought that would please their pretend gods, but instead it made the real God **very angry** indeed.

"These people are **so cruel**," He said. "It is time I gave their land to the Jews, just as I have always **promised.**"

"They're coming!"

screamed the Canaanites one day.

"Look at the dust cloud out in the desert.

But they'll **never** get over the River Jordan," they told each other.

"It's far too deep and wide."

But as they watched the priests carry a golden box into the water, the river

stopped flowing and all the Jews

walked through the riverbed,
just as God had told them.

"Run into Jericho!"

shouted the Canaanites. "The walls of the city

are **so thick** we'll be **safe** there."

As the huge, iron gates slammed shut they felt much better, and when nothing happened for a while, the Canaanites

began to laugh!

"They're scared!" they said. But they were wrong. The Jews had learned to trust God in those forty long years in the desert, and they were just waiting for Him to tell them what to do next. Joshua was their leader now that Moses had died, and the people knew that God was with him.

Of course there was no way **they** could ever get into Jericho; those walls were **far too strong**. But God had a plan for them. Early one morning the Canaanites were awakened by a **strange sound.**

"The Jews are marching around our city," they said, "carrying a golden box and blowing their trumpets!"

Every day for a week the same thing happened and the Canaanites began to get nervous.

"What are they trying to do?" they whispered.

On the **seventh** day God told the Jews to march around Jericho, not once, but *seven* times.

Then they had to make as much noise as they possibly could. As they SHOUTED and blew their horns, the great city walls began to rattle and shake, and enormous cracks appeared between the bricks.

The Canaanites were horrified.

Then, with a terrible, rumbling crash, the walls collapsed, all the way around the city. The people inside were much too frightened to fight, and all the Jews had to do was walk in and capture Jericho.

After many battles and great adventures, the whole land was theirs.

With God's help the entire land of Canaan belonged to Israel—just as He had promised.

"This is lovely!" they said as they looked at the green fields and juicy fruit.

Joshua told the priests to set up the tent for worshiping God on top of a high hill.

Then he called everyone together and said, "God has been good to you. Now that you are safely here, will you continue to love and obey Him?"

"Of course we will!"

the people shouted.

"And you won't start worshiping pretend gods like the Canaanites did?" persisted Joshua.

"NEVER!" they all replied.

How happy they all were as long as they kept that promise.

Let's talk about the story

1. The Jews had to wander in the desert for a very long time. Why? What had they done?

2. What very important lesson did the Jews learn in the desert?

3. How did the Jews conquer Jericho? What was God's plan?

4. Have you ever had a problem so big that you knew you couldn't solve it yourself? What did you do?

5. What are some situations that you have to trust God to take care of?